animal attack!

LION ATTACKS

Patrick J. Fitzgerald

HIGH interest **books**

Children's Press
A Division of Grolier Publishing
New York / London / Hong Kong / Sydney
Danbury, Connecticut

To my wife, Wendy

Book Design: Kim M. Sonsky
Contributing Editor: Jennifer Ceaser

Photo Credits: pp. 4, 6, 39 © Digital Vision; pp. 9, 11 © Digital Stock; pp. 13, 31 ©
Joe McDonald/Corbis; p. 14 © Yann Arthus-Bertrand/Corbis; p. 16 © O. Alamany and
E. Vicens/Corbis; p. 19 © Peter Johnson/Corbis; pp. 23, 26 The Everett Collection; pp.
28, 34, 36 © AP/Wide World Photos; p. 33 © Dean Conger/Corbis.

Visit Children's Press on the Internet at:
http://publishing.grolier.com

Library of Congress Cataloging-in-Publication Data

Fitzgerald, Patrick J., 1966–
    Lion Attacks / Patrick Fitzgerald.
        p. cm. – (Animal attacks)
    Includes bibliographical references (p. 44).
    Summary: Discusses the history of lion attacks on humans and the reasons for the
    attacks, including species endangerment, loss of habitat, and dangers of captivity.
    ISBN 0-516-23315-7 (lib. bdg) – ISBN 0-516-23515-x (pbk)
    1. Lion Attacks–Juvenile literature. 2. Lions–Juvenile literature. [1. Lions.] I. Title.
    II. Series.

QL737.C23 F58 2000
599.757'1566–dc21   99-054151

contents

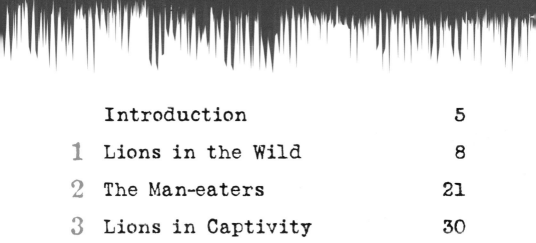

introduction

He is the ruler of the jungle and the king of the beasts. He is the lion—one of the fiercest of the world's big cats.

Up until 10,000 years ago, lions lived all over the world. They could be found throughout Africa and North America and in parts of Europe, the Middle East, and India. Today, wild lions can be found only in protected game preserves in Africa and India. Two types of lions live on these preserves: the African lion and the Asiatic lion. The African lion lives in central and southern Africa, in an area near the Sahara desert. Only a few hundred lions still live in India. They are all that

The male lion is easily recognized by his mane.

Introduction

remain of the Asiatic lion family. In the last few decades, both African and Asiatic lions have lost most of their habitat. A habitat is an area where an animal naturally lives and grows. Humans have taken over much of the lion's habitat to build houses, roads, and office buildings.

As people have moved into the lions' territory, the number of lion attacks on humans has increased. Most lion attacks occur on game preserves or in villages near the preserves. Many attacks also take place in circuses and zoos.

Lions do not attack humans as often as do tigers. Yet when lions attack, they are more aggressive and more likely to kill. Legend has it that once a lion has tasted human flesh, it will become a regular man-eater.

A female African lion with her cub

chapter one

LIONS IN THE WILD

It was a warm April evening in South Africa's Kruger National Park. Two park rangers, Ginneth Maganyi and Thomas Chauke, were out for a jog. The men knew the danger of being attacked by a wild animal. They both were armed with rifles. As they jogged through the northern area of the park, Maganyi was suddenly knocked to the ground. Before he realized what was happening, he felt a burning pain in his neck. An enormous male lion had pinned him down and was biting and tearing at his neck and head. Maganyi struggled to reach his weapon. Chauke acted quickly, shooting the lion dead and saving his fellow ranger's life.

A lion may spend up to 20 hours a day resting.

LION ATTACKS

Harold Braack, a ranger at the park, told the Pretoria News, *"It appears the lion stalked one of the two and attacked him." Braack reported that the attacker was an old male lion that was obviously starving. Braack went on to explain that it is normal for an older lion to attack slower animals. In this case, the slow-moving animal was a man.*

The lion deserves to be called one of Earth's most powerful predators. Lions are second in size only to tigers. A full-grown male lion is a big animal. He is about 4 feet (121 cm) high and between 6 and 7 feet (183–213 cm) long. He can weigh up to 500 pounds (225 kg). A female lion, or lioness, is smaller. Her body is about 5 feet (152 cm) long and 3½ feet (107 cm) high. A lioness weighs between 265 and 390 pounds (119–175 kg). Lions can jump as high as 7 feet (213 cm) and as far as 30 feet (914 cm). They can run for short distances at up to 35 miles (56 km) per hour.

A male lion is a large animal that can weigh 500 pounds (225 kg).

A PRIDE'S TERRITORY

Lions are the only big cats that live in groups, called prides. A pride is similar to a large family. A pride is made up of several generations of lionesses and their babies, called cubs. One or two male lions also live with the pride. The males' job is to protect the pride's territory and to mate with the females.

A pride may have as few as four and as many as thirty-seven members. The average number of lions in a pride is about fifteen. Each pride has a specific territory. The size of the territory depends on the amount of prey in it. A pride's territory may be as small as 8 square miles (20 sq. km) when there is a lot of prey available. When prey is hard to find, a pride's territory becomes as large as 150 square miles (388 sq. km).

HUNTING AND EATING

Lions are carnivores, or meat-eaters. Lions usually hunt at night. They eat all kinds of animals of all different sizes. Their favorite food is medium- to

Zebras make up a large part of the lion's diet.

large-size animals with hooves, such as antelope and zebra. Lions also will eat carrion, or animals that are already dead. They will regularly steal food from other predators, such as hyenas. There aren't many predators on the plains of Africa that want to fight with a lion.

Lionesses do most of the killing. A lioness can bring down a large animal, such as a wildebeest.

The members of a pride spend the day in several small groups. If there is plenty of prey available, lions will spend up to 20 hours a day resting and sleeping. Then the small groups will come together at night to hunt or share in a kill.

When hunting, the job of the male lion is to drive the prey to waiting female lions. Lionesses do most of the actual killing. They often hunt in groups, unlike male lions, which hunt alone. The female lions work together by quietly circling a herd of animals.

They use every available piece of ground cover to hide in, such as tall grasses. Then the lionesses close in for the kill. They run down their prey in a short burst of speed and then leap onto the animal's back. A lioness is so strong that she can tackle an animal twice her weight to the ground. Her powerful jaws lock onto the victim's neck. She rips at its throat until it is strangled. Then she begins to eat the animal, starting with its intestines and working her way out. Sometimes, the victim is not dead when the rest of the pride gathers around to begin eating.

Male lions get most of the meat from the kill. After the males are finished, the lionesses move in to eat. The cubs are last and get

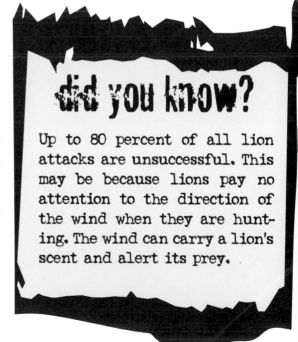

did you know?

Up to 80 percent of all lion attacks are unsuccessful. This may be because lions pay no attention to the direction of the wind when they are hunting. The wind can carry a lion's scent and alert its prey.

Lions rest their heads on the remains of their kill.

the smallest amount. An adult male typically eats 75 pounds (34 kg) of meat in one meal. Adult lions stuff themselves on the fresh kill. Then they rest anywhere from several days to one week before they start hunting again.

WHY LIONS ATTACK

Lions in the wild usually will run away when they see or hear people. However, a lion will attack a human for several reasons:

- It may be defending its territory or looking for a new one.
- It could be protecting a fresh kill, and a person has come too close to it.
- It might be starving.
- It could be old, injured, or sick and no longer able to hunt its normal prey (the most common reason).

When People Get Too Close

In the last few years, much of the Asiatic lion's game preserve in India's Gir Forest has disappeared. The land has been cleared to make way for farms, ranches, and roads. Many attacks on humans have occurred because the lions have so little territory left.

In a ten-year period, from 1977 to 1987, there

did you know?

Roaring is how lions declare their territory. A roar can be heard from as far away as 5 miles (8 km). The lion usually roars in the evening just before the night's hunting begins. Lions also roar in the morning, just before dawn.

were sixty-five lion attacks in and around the game preserve. Eight people died from the attacks. By the end of 1987, the lions' territory was reduced to just 134 square miles (347 sq. km). The area was no longer large enough to support the lions. They were forced to go outside the preserve to look for food. In just twenty-seven months, from January 1988 to April 1990, there was a huge increase in the number of lion attacks on humans. There were eighty-one attacks, resulting in sixteen deaths. Before 1987, lions attacked an average of six people each year. After 1987, there was an average of three lion attacks each month!

Lions will use the roads that cross through their hunting grounds.

Most of the lion attacks took place near farms and ranches. These are places where humans and cattle live close together. The lions were most likely hunting cows until they realized that humans were easier to catch. Since people were living so close to the lions, the big cats may have lost their fear of humans.

Dangerous Travel

In many game preserves, roads cross through lions' hunting grounds. The roads are used to carry tourists, but many people also use them for regular travel. Villagers often walk or ride bikes through the game preserve, going from their small towns to large outdoor markets. They load up with food and go back home along the roads. Lions have learned that the villagers are easy prey. "A person traveling on a bike looks no different than an antelope to a lion," one of the park's rangers explained to a London newspaper, the *Electronic Telegraph.*

Lions also use the roads to their advantage when hunting. They often chase their prey toward the hard surface, where the animal is more likely to trip and break a leg. The injured animal is far easier for the lion to capture. Often the lion will not bother to drag the animal's dead body off the road. The lion stays near its catch, protecting it from scavengers. Anyone walking along the road, especially at night, runs a great risk of coming between a lion and its kill. The lion will attack anything, including a human being, to defend its catch.

chapter two

THE MAN-EATERS

One Saturday morning in July 1998, South African soldiers were on regular patrol in the Kruger National Park. It was a day they would not soon forget.

As the soldiers marched through the high grass of the game preserve, they stumbled across the body of a woman. It was clear that she had been attacked and partly eaten by a lion. Her intestines had been torn from her stomach. The back of her head and legs had also been chewed away.

"The woman's face was easily identified since it was not eaten," a park police captain told the South African newspaper The Star. *The woman was trying*

to cross into South Africa illegally from Mozambique. Thousands of Mozambican citizens cross the park every year looking for work in South Africa.

The attack on the woman was the second in the park in one week. It was the fourth attack reported in six months. In an earlier attack, an eleven-year-old Mozambican girl, Emelda Anja Nkuna, was found wandering alone in the park. A pack of lions had killed her entire family. Emelda had hidden in a hole, watching as lions attacked her mother and two sisters. Rangers were unable to find any trace of the girl's sisters following the attack. Only the mother's head was found.

Similar attacks have occurred in nearby Uganda, where a pride of lions killed at least sixteen people. Experts on lion behavior say that the lions responsible for the attacks in Uganda and in Kruger National Park are not vicious killers. Instead, these experts blame humans for taking over the lion's natural habitat. Lions have found

When lions attack, they often grab their victim by
the neck and tear at the throat.

humans wandering on foot to be much easier to
hunt and capture.

"The problem is not the lions, but illegal immi-
grants," Dr. Willem Gertenbach, the Kruger
National Park general manager, told *The Star*.
"There is a very good possibility that many more
[Mozambicans] have died because sometimes we
find abandoned luggage and torn clothes, but we
don't find bodies."

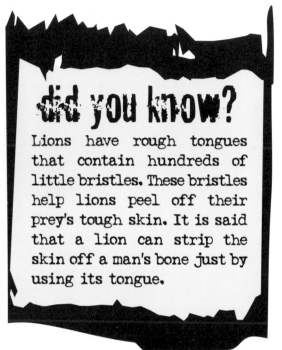

did you know?

Lions have rough tongues that contain hundreds of little bristles. These bristles help lions peel off their prey's tough skin. It is said that a lion can strip the skin off a man's bone just by using its tongue.

After several more Mozambicans were killed in a three-week period, park officials had to kill seven of the man-eating lions. When they examined one lion's stomach, they found human feet, fingers, and tongues.

THE MAN-EATERS OF TSAVO

More than one hundred years ago, two male lions terrorized an area near the Tsavo River in Africa. It is one of the most famous man-eating incidents of all time. By the time the pair was done, it is estimated that they had killed 140 people.

The trouble all began in 1898, when the British government decided to build a railroad in East Africa. British Colonel John Henry Patterson was put in charge of building a bridge over the Tsavo River. Soon after Patterson arrived in early March, workers began to disappear from the camps around the construction site. The terrified men told Patterson that two male lions were responsible for the deaths. The men believed that the lions lived in a cave near the Tsavo River. The men refused to return to work until Patterson had the lions killed. Construction on the railroad stopped.

One night, one of the lions attacked one of the camp's tents. It grabbed a man right out of his bed, dragged him off, and ate him. The next night, the other lion attacked the hospital tent. The men saw the lion sink its teeth into a hospital worker and pull him from the tent. The next day, all they could find of the worker was his head and part of his hand. Another night, the lions dragged their victim close to Patterson's tent. Patterson described the sounds he heard as the lions ate the man: There was the loud crunch of human bones, followed by satisfied growling.

A lion will attack anything, even a person, when it is hungry.

It was early 1899, and the killings had been going on for ten months. Patterson still couldn't stop the man-eating lions from attacking. He had fired off several shots at the lions, but he always missed. The workers began to think of the lions as devils. Every night men in the camps heard roaring. Suddenly, the roaring would stop. Word went from camp to camp, "Beware—the devils are coming!" Then the men heard terrified screams coming from somewhere in the camp. At roll call in the morning, one more worker would be missing.

Finally, Colonel Patterson was able to kill one of the lions, using a donkey as bait. One week later, Patterson killed the other lion. It took six bullets to kill the second man-eater of Tsavo.

The men finally were able to finish building the bridge. The skins and skulls of the lions were shipped to America. The lions are stuffed and on display at the Field Museum of Natural History in Chicago, Illinois. The story of the Tsavo man-eaters is so famous that it inspired the 1996 movie *The Ghost and the Darkness*.

Although male lions rarely hunt in pairs, it is not unheard of. No one knows for certain what turned this pair into man-eaters. Some scientists say the lions may have learned the behavior from their mother. Others believe that the lions were driven to attack because they were starving.

A lion will attack for many reasons. Here, a lioness defends her territory against an unlucky zookeeper.

MODERN MAN-EATERS

Man-eaters are not just a thing of the past, however. In August 1999, nineteen-year-old David Pleydell-Souverie was asleep in his tent in a national park in

Zimbabwe, Africa. An injured lioness, with the help of a male lion, dragged the teenager from his tent. His screams woke nearby campers who immediately alerted the park guards. Nothing was found of Pleydell-Souverie; the lions had eaten his entire body.

Park officials tracked down and shot the lion and lioness responsible for the attack. When they opened the animals' stomachs, they found clothing belonging to Pleydell-Souverie.

A representative from Zambesi Safari and Travel told the news service *Electronic Telegraph*; "The lioness is quite well-known. She used to have an abscess (infection) on her foot, which was treated by park officials. But her leg may have been broken later. Lions only attack humans if they have been injured and are unable to hunt for their normal prey."

chapter three

LIONS IN CAPTIVITY

David Windell was spending an enjoyable weekend afternoon with his grandson. They were visiting a game farm in South Africa. The two-year-old boy was standing at the fence of a lion pen while his grandfather looked on. Suddenly, a young lioness leaped toward the toddler. The lioness was able to grab the boy's leg through a small gap under the fence. As she started to drag the screaming boy into the pen, his grandfather quickly acted.

"I had the lioness by the nose, and I was trying to twist its nose so it would let him go," Windell told the African newspaper The Citizen. *"Any grandfather*

Because lions are wild animals, even those raised in captivity may attack.

would have done the same thing." A park ranger jumped on the lioness from behind. He began kicking the lioness until she released the boy. Windell then pulled his grandson to safety.

The toddler had an emergency operation and survived. He was lucky to be attacked by a young lion. If it had been an adult lion, the boy would not have survived. Even so, the boy received sixty stitches in his right leg.

Like most animals in zoos, the young lioness in the attack had been born and raised in captivity. Animals who live in captivity have never lived in the wild. They depend on humans to feed them and have not learned to hunt. Lions in captivity are much less likely to attack people than those in the wild. Yet even in captivity, lion attacks occur.

"You're dealing with a wild animal," a South African park ranger explained to *The Star*. "There is always some level of danger. And any lion that loses its fear of humans becomes a potential man-eater."

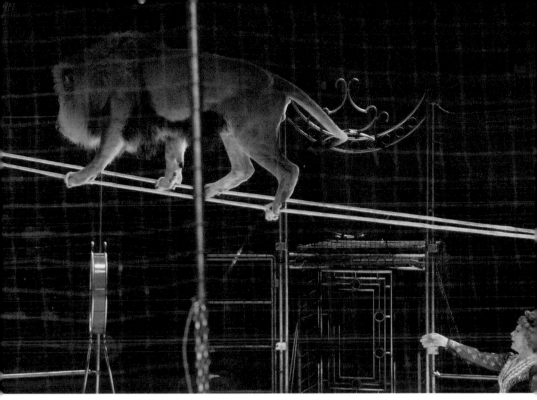

A lion performs as its tamer stands nearby.

LIONS IN CIRCUSES

In 1993, Graham Chipperfield was working as a lion tamer with the Ringling Bros. and Barnum & Bailey Circus. During a training session, a male lion attacked the tamer. Chipperfield suffered deep wounds to his face and arms. Just three days earlier, another lion had injured a Ringling Bros. trainer. The trainer had been breaking up a fight between two lions.

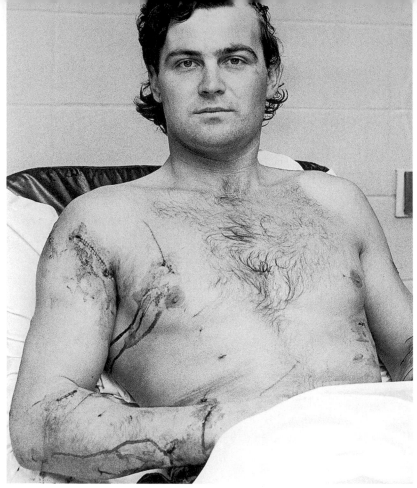

This trainer was attacked by Prince, a male lion in Zerbini's Circus, during a performance.

In 1991, at a Kessler Bros. Circus performance, a lioness turned on her trainer. People watched in horror as the lioness took her trainer's head in her mouth and slowly suffocated him. The lioness was shot to death, but not before the trainer had died.

Attacks on circus workers usually occur if a lion feels threatened or trapped. A lion also may react to a loud noise or a sudden movement, such as that made with a whip. A lion may attack a trainer if it decides the person has gotten too close for comfort.

LIONS IN ZOOS

Lion attacks in zoos are rare. They occur much less often than tiger attacks, for instance. Most lion attacks occur when a zookeeper is cleaning an animal's living area. This kind of attack happened at the North Carolina Zoo in 1998. Two lions attacked a keeper who was cleaning their enclosure. One lion grabbed the keeper by the legs. The other lion clamped its jaws around the man's head. The zookeeper received deep bite wounds

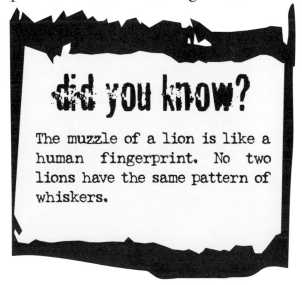

did you know?

The muzzle of a lion is like a human fingerprint. No two lions have the same pattern of whiskers.

A likely target for a lion attack is a zookeeper. A lion may feel that a zookeeper is invading its territory.

on his head and legs before he could be rescued.

Other attacks occur when visitors enter a lion's territory. Lions killed a woman after she climbed into their enclosure at the National Zoo in Washington, D.C. Her body was so bruised and shredded that her fingerprints and face could not be recognized.

A WILD ANIMAL, NOT A PET

Other attacks occur when people decide to raise or breed big cats. They build enclosures for lions and tigers in their yards. Usually, the people are not qualified to take care of big cats. Often, the pens they have built for the animals are not secure.

In 1995, a Louisiana woman was visiting the home of a friend who collected big cats. The woman decided to get a closer look at the lion and entered its cage. The woman's nine-year-old daughter watched in horror as her mother was ripped apart by the friend's "pet" lion. The friend was also seriously injured as he tried to stop the killing.

A similar incident took place in 1997. A lion and a tiger attacked a thirteen-year-old boy as he entered their enclosure. The animals were kept as caged "pets" in his grandfather's yard. "My boy was not mauled," the grandfather told the Caldwell, Texas, newspaper. "He was being eaten alive."

chapter four

THREATS TO SURVIVAL

Lions aren't an endangered species, but lion populations in India and Africa are being threatened. There are fewer lions in these countries because people have destroyed much of the cats' natural habitat. As their territory shrinks, lions have fewer animals on which to prey. Hungry lions must look elsewhere for food. The lions are at the risk of being shot because they eat villagers' livestock.

Disease is another reason why the lion population is at risk. In the last few years, more than one thousand lions in Tanzania's Serengeti National Park have died from a disease carried by pet dogs in nearby villages.

To make sure that lions will continue to live into the next century, humans need to balance their demand for land with protection of the lion's habitat. Organizations such as the American Zoo and Aquarium Association work to help increase the lion population. Game reserves such as Tanzania's Serengeti National Park and Zimbabwe's Matusadona National Park have helped to save lions and other threatened species. With more research and understanding, the lion can continue to live as the king of the beasts— in the wild, where it belongs.

FACT SHEET

African lion Species of lion living in Africa.
panthera leo The scientific (Latin) name for the
   African lion.
Asiatic lion Species of lion living in India.
panthera leo persica The scientific (Latin) name for
   the Asiatic lion.
simba The Swahili word for lion.

*In the wild, lions live on the following game preserves
in Africa and India*:

   Gir Forest Sanctuary, India (Asiatic lions live
   here)
   Kruger National Park, South Africa
   Matusadona National Park, Zimbabwe
   Queen Elizabeth National Park, Uganda
   Serengeti National Park, Tanzania

Life span

Between eight and ten years in the wild
Up to twenty-five years in captivity

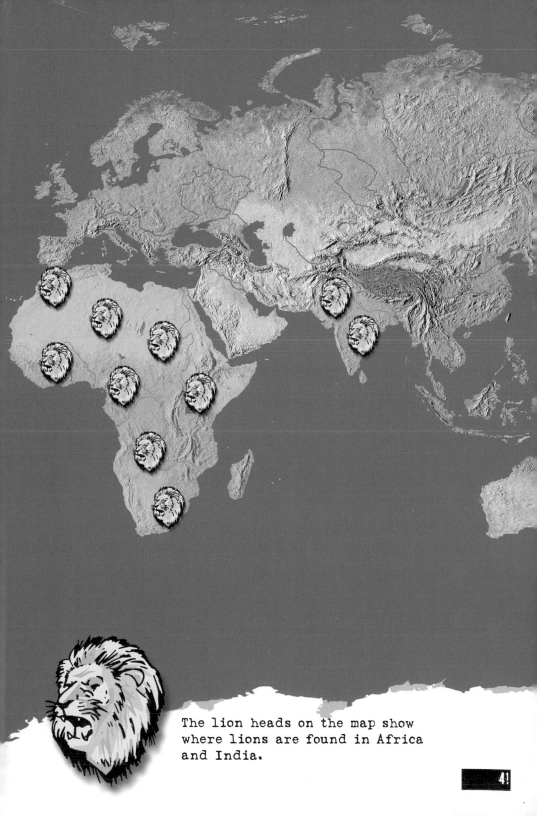

The lion heads on the map show
where lions are found in Africa
and India.

new words

captivity not living in the wild; living in an enclosure

carnivore an animal that eats meat

carrion an animal that is already dead

conservation the careful protection of animals

cub a baby lion

enclosure an area where an animal is kept, a pen or cage

endangered threatened with extinction

game preserve a place where animals are protected from hunters

habitat an area where an animal naturally lives and grows

hyena a small, meat-eating scavenger

lion tamer a person who trains and performs with lions, usually for a circus

lioness a female lion

livestock animals bred and raised by man for food and work, such as cows

mane the fringe of hair around a male lion's face and head

predator an animal that hunts and kills other
  animals

prey an animal that is killed and eaten for food

pride an extended family of lions

scavenger an animal or bird that feeds on a dead or
  decaying animal

territory an area that is occupied and defended by
  an animal or group of animals

for further reading

Adamson, Joy. *Born Free: A Lioness of Two Worlds.*
   New York: Pantheon, 1987.

Capstick, Peter Hathaway. *Maneaters.* Los Angeles:
   Peterson Publishing Co., 1993.

Iwago, Mitsuaki. *In the Lion's Den.* San Francisco:
   Chronicle Books, 1996.

Spies, Dr. Joseph R. *Big Cats and Other Animals:
   Their Beauty, Dignity, and Survival.* Hollywood,
   FL: Lifetime Books, Inc., 1998.

American Zoo and Aquarium Association
P.O. Box 79863
Baltimore, MD 21279
Web site: *www.aza.org*
Has links to local national zoos and aquariums. Tells what each organization is doing to save endangered species. Includes information about AZA programs as well as research links and a photo gallery.

Animal Attack Files
http://www.igorilla.com/gorilla/animal/
This site offers a great selection of news articles describing recent attacks on humans by animals.

Asiatic Lion Information Centre
http://wk.web4.cableinet.co.uk/alic/
General facts about the Asiatic lion, including information about its habitat and threats to its survival. Provides current updates about the Asiatic lion and information about lion conservation programs.

Big Cats Online

http://dialspace.dial.pipex.com/agarman/
This site gives profiles of all the big cats, including
facts about their evolution. It also gives information
on worldwide conservation efforts for each species.

World Wildlife Fund—United States

1250 24th Street, NW
Washington, DC 20037-1175
Web site: *www.worldwildlife.org*
Dedicated to the conservation of endangered and
threatened species. Includes the latest news relating
to conservation efforts. Has information about their
programs and how to get involved. Also sponsors the
Conservation Action Network, an online chat room
where people discuss conservation issues.

index

About the Author

Patrick J. Fitzgerald is a freelance writer who has had a lifelong interest in big cats. He lives in Brooklyn, NY, with his wife Wendy, two cats, and his dog.